GCSE ENGLISH LITERATURE

Skills & Practice

for OCR

Steven Croft

OCR
RECOGNISING ACHIEVEMENT
OXFORD
UNIVERSITY PRESS

Official Publisher Partnership

OxBox

OXFORD
UNIVERSITY PRESS

Oxford University Press is a department of the University of Oxford. It furthers
the University's objective of excellence in research, scholarship, and education
by publishing worldwide in

Oxford   New York

Auckland   Cape Town   Dar es Salaam   Hong Kong   Karachi
Kuala Lumpur   Madrid   Melbourne   Mexico City   Nairobi
New Delhi   Shanghai   Taipei   Toronto

With offices in

Argentina   Austria   Brazil   Chile   Czech Republic   France   Greece
Guatemala   Hungary   Italy   Japan   South Korea   Poland   Portugal   Singapore
Switzerland   Thailand   Turkey   Ukraine   Vietnam

Oxford is a registered trade mark of Oxford University Press
in the UK and in certain other countries

British Library Cataloguing in Publication Data
Data available

ISBN: 978-0-19-913885-2

10 9 8 7 6 5 4 3 2 1

Printed in Great Britain by Ashford Colour Press Ltd., Gosport.

Acknowledgements

The authors and publisher are grateful for permission to reprint the
following copyright material:

Carol Ann Duffy: 'Anne Hathaway' from *The World's Wife* (Picador, 2010),
copyright © Carol Ann Duffy 1999, reprinted by permission of Pan
Macmillan, London.

Elizabeth Jennings: 'My Grandmother' from *Collected Poems 1953-1985*
(Carcanet, 1987), reprinted by permission of David Higham Associates Ltd.

Harper Lee: extract from *To Kill a Mockingbird* (Wm Heinemann 1960/Vintage
2004), reprinted by permission of The Random House Group Ltd.

John Steinbeck: extract from *Of Mice and Men* (Penguin, 2006), copyright ©
John Steinbeck 1937, 1965, reprinted by permission of Penguin Books Ltd.

Although we have made every effort to trace and contact all copyright
holders before publication this has not been possible in all cases. If notified,
the publisher will rectify any errors or omissions at the earliest opportunity.

Illustrations by Q2A.

Contents

Preparing for Assessment

To do well in your English Literature GCSE it is important that you understand what each element of your course involves so that you can prepare for it carefully. Your assessment consists of four units:

Unit 1 (A661): Literary Heritage Linked Texts (Controlled Assessment)
Unit 2 (A662): Modern Drama (45 minutes written exam)
Unit 3 (A663): Prose from Different Cultures (45 minutes written exam)
Unit 4 (A664): Literary Heritage Prose and Contemporary Poetry (1 hour 30 minutes written exam)

Preparing for the written exams

The written exams make up 75% of your total marks for GCSE.

I. Planning and preparing

Careful planning and preparation is essential if you are to be successful in your exams. Some of this preparation will take place throughout the course and some of it in the weeks immediately before you take your exams.

Throughout the course
- Read widely around the texts you are studying and read as wide a variety of poetry as you can.
- Wide reading will help you improve your own vocabulary, sentence structures and understanding of how texts of different kinds are written and organised.
- When you read different kinds of texts, think carefully about how writers use language in different ways to create particular effects.

Planning your revision
- Begin your revision in good time.
- Devise a revision timetable.
- Make sure that you know exactly what to expect on each of your exam papers. Look at past papers and at the sample questions in this book (as well as your Student Book). Practise answering these questions in the same amount of time that you will have in each exam.
- Look at the mark schemes for your exam papers – these will show you what the examiners are looking for. (Ask your teacher about them or you can look on the examination board's website.)

2. The question paper

You will save yourself time if you know what to expect on each question paper. You can find key information about each question paper in the **insight** section at the start of each unit.

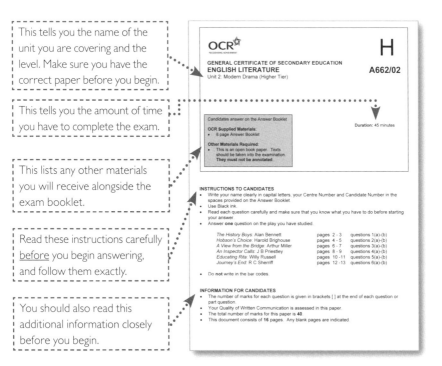

This tells you the name of the unit you are covering and the level. Make sure you have the correct paper before you begin.

This tells you the amount of time you have to complete the exam.

This lists any other materials you will receive alongside the exam booklet.

Read these instructions carefully before you begin answering, and follow them exactly.

You should also read this additional information closely before you begin.

3. Planning and checking your answers

- Make sure you that you read all of the questions before you start to write anything.
- Set aside at least five minutes before you begin writing to think about and plan your answer. Careful planning is essential if you are to produce the best answer you can.
- Plan using notes – don't waste time writing in full sentences.
- Leave yourself a few minutes at the end of the exam to check your spelling, punctuation, grammar and paragraphing and that you have done everything the question asks.

4. Aiming for A*

To achieve a top grade you must be able to:
- structure your answer well and write clearly and fluently
- use accurate spelling, punctuation and grammar

- show that you have an overview of each text or theme and the ability to move from more general ideas to specific points
- convey your ideas persuasively and coherently using relevant evidence from the texts to support your points.

Preparing for Controlled Assessment

What is Controlled Assessment?

Controlled Assessment is a way of assessing your work in a controlled situation which is not a formal exam. In units assessed by Controlled Assessment you will have to complete tasks set by the exam board and your work will be marked by your teacher before being moderated by OCR.

Unit 1 of your English Literature GCSE is assessed by Controlled Assessment; partly through written tasks and partly through speaking and listening tasks. Altogether Controlled Assessment will make up 25% of your total English Literature GCSE mark.

The stages of Controlled Assessment

Controlled Assessment takes place in three stages:

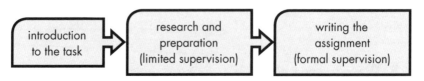

introduction to the task → research and preparation (limited supervision) → writing the assignment (formal supervision)

Introduction to the task
Your teacher will introduce you to the task and make sure that you know exactly what to do and what is required of you.

Research and preparation
During this part of the process you will be able to work under 'limited supervision' which means that you will be able to work without being directly supervised. You may be able to work with other students and some of your work might be done outside the classroom.

Writing your assignment

This is where you write your final piece of work or take part in the speaking and listening activity. You may be asked to complete your written assignment in one session or your writing time may be split over several sessions. This stage will be completed under 'formal supervision' which means you will be supervised at all times and will not be allowed to use reference materials, other than your own notes, or to discuss your work with other students.

I. Preparing the task

Once your teacher has introduced the task you will spend some time researching and preparing for Controlled Assessment. During this time your teacher will be able to discuss the task with you, but can only give you general advice.

During this stage of the assessment you should:
- plan how you are going to approach the task
- research your topic to inform and develop your own ideas
- organize and structure your ideas
- keep a record of all research materials you have used so far and where you found them.

2. Writing your response

You will write your assessment under formal supervision.
Remember to:
- do everything the task asks you to do
- write in Standard English using full sentences and paragraphs – do not write in note form
- keep track of the time and leave yourself enough time at the end to read through and check your work
- be careful to acknowledge all sources and quotations that you use.

3. Checking your work

Make sure that you read your work before handing it in. You should check that:
- you have not made any errors in spelling or punctuation
- you have used sentences and paragraphs correctly
- you have not made any grammatical mistakes
- you have done everything that the task requires.

4. Boost your grade

To achieve a top grade in your assessment you must be able to:
- show that you have a clear understanding of the demands of the task
- show that you have an overview of the texts you are focusing on
- structure your answer well and write clearly and fluently
- write technically accurate English in terms of grammar, punctuation and spelling
- use effective, well-chosen vocabulary
- convey your ideas coherently and persuasively using relevant evidence from the texts to support your ideas.

Key skills

Technical errors in your writing can cost you precious marks and might prevent you achieving a grade C or above. During your course you need to do all you can to improve the standard of your written English. You can do this by:
- being aware of the kinds of mistakes you often make
- taking note of your teacher's corrections
- making a note of any particular words you spell incorrectly or punctuation marks you have problems with
- working on the areas you know cause you problems
- checking your work through carefully.

Technical errors usually fall into three main categories:
1. spelling
2. punctuation
3. grammar.

This section outlines some common problem areas, and helps you revise the basic skills necessary for success at GCSE.

Preparing for Assessment

I. Spelling

If you have some difficulties with spelling it does not mean that you will not pass your GCSE but it could prevent you achieving high marks.

Here are some things you can do to improve your spelling skills:
- Read as much as possible – seeing words in print can help you visualise them as you write.
- Identify the words that you frequently spell incorrectly and make a list of them.
- Work at learning these words and devise strategies such as rhymes to help you, for example, for 'receive': *i before e except after c.*
- Get into the habit of reading through your written work and checking it carefully for mistakes.

Here are some words that are commonly misspelt. Look at them carefully and see if you can identify what is wrong with each one.

Now, write down the correct spelling of each word. If you do not know what the word means, look it up in a dictionary and write the meaning down next to the correct spelling.

begining	soliloqueys	metaphores
onomatopoia	oximoron	caracters
similie	comparisen	stansa
rythm	ryme	aliteration
playright	antiphesis	parralel
cesura	coloquial	monolog
conotation	narative	sonnett

Keep your own list of words that you sometimes misspell and watch out for these words in your own writing.

Commonly confused words

Some spelling mistakes happen because one word has been confused with a similar word. The next page contains some words that are commonly confused.

you're – your
- You're going to be in trouble if you do that.
- I like your new bike.

know – now – no
- I know you can do this.
- It is time to leave now.
- We have no homework today.

being – been
- You are being very annoying.
- I have been such a fool!

loose – lose
- That knot is coming loose.
- Don't lose the money I gave you.

where – wear – were
- Where did I put my bag?
- I don't know what I am going to wear for the party.
- They were really looking forward to the holidays.

The list below includes more words that are often confused. Make sure that you know what they mean and when to use them. Try writing a sentence of your own using each one.

affect/effect	accept/except	all ready/already
breathe/breath	practise/practice	sight/site
council/counsel	past/passed	principle/principal
stationary/stationery	through/threw	imminent/eminent

---

2. Punctuation

Like spelling, correct punctuation is important if you are to achieve the grade you are capable of. Be aware of any particular kinds of punctuation that you have problems with and work on improving your skills.

Here are some key punctuation marks you should make sure you use accurately in your writing:
- full stops
- question marks
- speech marks
- apostrophes.

Full stops

Sentences end with a full stop, but how you divide your writing up into sentences depends to some extent on what you are writing about and the effects you want to achieve. Remember that all sentences should make sense individually. Another common mistake is to string together completed statements with commas instead of using full stops to separate them.

Question marks

You will probably be quite clear about where to use question marks, but the main problem students have is remembering to put them in – particularly when writing under pressure. Remember:
• do not put a full stop and a question mark together
• do not use a question mark in a sentence that is an indirect question.

Look at the two sentences below. One of them is an example of a direct question and the other an indirect question. Which do you think needs a question mark?

1. *Have you finished your revision programme*
2. *She asked me if I had finished my revision programme*

Speech marks

Remember these key points when using speech marks:
• only put the speech marks around the words actually spoken (not the part that tells you who is speaking)
• other punctuation marks relating to what is actually said, such as question marks or exclamation marks, go <u>inside</u> the speech marks
• when two or more people are speaking, remember to start a new line each time a different person speaks.

Apostrophes

Apostrophes are used for two main reasons:

- They can be used to show where letters have been missed out in shortening words or running two words together (these are called 'contractions'), e.g. *you are – you're; we had – we'd.*
- They can be used to show that something belongs to someone or something (these are possessive apostrophes). Watch out for **its** and **it's**: here *it's* is a contraction of *it is*, while *its* is a possessive form indicating something belonging to 'it', e.g. *The dog ate its food.*

3. Grammar

Grammatical errors can make your work harder to read and your meaning less clear. Always check your written work through carefully for grammatical mistakes. If you can, read your work aloud – if it sounds wrong then it probably is wrong. Here are two common mistakes.

Changing tense

Inconsistency in the use of tense can sometimes cause problems for students. Sometimes tenses are incorectly switched within a paragraph or sometimes even within a sentence.

For example:
Sue ran as fast as she could but missed her bus. She sits down and starts to cry.

Sue ran as fast as she could but missed her bus: This is written in the past tense but the next sentence – *She sits down and starts to cry* – is written in the present tense. The two tenses should agree.

The correct version would read – *Sue ran as fast as she could but missed her bus. She sat down and started to cry.*

Always check your work to make sure that your tenses agree.

Could of, Would of, Should of

Muddling 'of' with 'have' is another common mistake because of the similarity in the way they sound. The correct way of writing these phrases is *could have, would have, should have.* For example: *Sue should have met Danny at six and she would have been early if she could have caught the bus.*

Controlled Assessment insight

Unit Summary

This unit is worth 25% of your overall GCSE English Literature mark. It is divided into two areas of study.

Unit 1: Literary Heritage Linked Texts

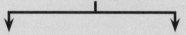

Shakespeare and film/audio/ live performance

You will study **one** Shakespeare play from the OCR list of plays and **one or two** film, audio or live performance(s) of the same play.

A task will be set on the play you have studied which will require you to write a critical analysis of the play and of linked scenes from the film, audio or live performance(s).

Literary Heritage Poetry

You will study **one** poet from a choice of six from the OCR list.

A task will be set on the poetry you have studied which will require you to compare **two** poems written by your chosen poet.

Shakespeare

You will study **one** of the following plays:
- *Julius Caesar*
- *Macbeth*
- *Merchant of Venice*
- *Romeo and Juliet*

Literary Heritage Poetry: OCR poetry anthology

You will study **one** of the following poets:
- Robert Browning
- Geoffrey Chaucer
- Thomas Hardy
- Wilfred Owen
- Christina Rossetti
- Shakespeare's Sonnets

Approaching the Controlled Assessment

This unit is assessed by Controlled Assessment. This means that you will be able to prepare for your tasks in lessons but you will write your final responses under formal supervision. The following points explain the stages of the Controlled Assessment.

1. Your Controlled Assessment will begin with a research and planning stage during which you will work under limited supervision. During this stage you will be able to work with other students and have access to reference materials.
2. You will then write your final assignment under formal supervision and are allowed up to **three** hours for each task.
3. For each piece you can write up to **1000 words**.
4. You are allowed to take unannotated copies of your texts and your own notes into the assessment with you.
5. You are also allowed access to dictionaries, thesauri and grammar and spell check programs.

Assessment Objectives

This unit will test the following Assessment Objectives:

AO1 Critical response to texts

AOI

Respond to texts critically and imaginatively; select and evaluate relevant textual detail to illustrate and support interpretations.

This means that you will need to show in your answer that you have read the texts closely and are able to analyse aspects such as the relationships, attitudes and motives of the characters. You will need to use carefully selected details from the text to illustrate and support your ideas.

AO3 Making links and comparisons

AO3

Make comparisons and explain links between texts, evaluating writers' different ways of expressing meaning and achieving effects.

This means that you will compare the ways in which writers have used language and different techniques to express meaning in the texts you have studied.

Studying your Shakespeare play

When approaching your play, remember that Shakespeare's plays, like any other plays, were written to be seen in performance, rather than read in a classroom. While reading the play always try to think about how it might work on stage.

One way you could approach the play in order to achieve a detailed understanding of it is given below.
- Read the whole play through carefully.
- If you can, read the play as a group.
- Make brief notes on each scene as you go through to help you develop on overall impression of the plot.
- Make notes on the characters and how they relate to each other.
- Imagine the action in your mind as you read each scene.
- List the key themes and ideas that are explored in the play.

Think about the play that you are studying, the ways in which characters and ideas are presented and the ways in which Shakespeare uses language to create his effects.

Write down all your ideas with examples and quotations.

Shakespeare's language

Shakespeare uses different forms of language at different points in the play. For example:
1. **Blank verse** – unrhymed verse using iambic pentameter (10 syllables a line consisting of an unstressed syllable followed by a stressed syllable). Much of Shakespeare's dramatic work consists of this form of verse.
2. **Rhymed verse** – this is often used at the end of scenes where rhyming couplets are used to draw the scene to a close. Rhymed verse is also sometimes used for dramatic effect.
3. **Prose** – is used in various contexts by characters of all kinds. It can be used to reveal heightened emotions, such as desperation, regret or grief; or to distinguish characters considered to be of a lower social status.

When commenting on Shakespeare's use of language, the key is to look at the specific context in which Shakespeare uses it. What is happening at that point in the play, and how does Shakespeare's choice of language help to convey meaning?

Literary Heritage Linked Texts

Shakespeare's imagery

Visual and aural imagery is very important in Shakespeare's plays. Often imagery is used to develop and reinforce important themes in the play or to characterise and present characters. Look carefully at the effects created through the use of:

- metaphors
- similes
- symbols and motifs
- alliteration
- assonance
- onomatopoeia.

Analysing characters

An essential part of your study of the play will be to understand how Shakespeare presents his characters.

You should consider all the points below when analysing character.
- Physical descriptions of characters – sometimes given in stage directions.
- What characters say and how they say it.
- What characters think (look for soliloquies and asides).
- How characters behave and respond to other characters.
- What is revealed about the motives of characters.
- How characters change (either in different situations or as the play goes on).

Soliloquies and asides

Make sure that you look carefully at all the soliloquies in your play. Shakespeare uses these as a means of revealing to the audience what is in the mind of a character. A soliloquy presents the character's dialogue as if they were speaking their thoughts aloud to the audience and so they are a good indication of the character's real feelings, plans or motivations.

Asides, although much shorter, are another device that allows Shakespeare to give the audience a true picture of a character's thoughts and feelings.

Draw up a table of the key characters in your play and for each one make a list of their key features or characteristics using evidence from the play to support and illustrate your ideas.

Identify the soliloquies in the play and make notes on what characters reveal in each soliloquy.

The play in performance

When you have arrived at a thorough and detailed understanding of your play you should then turn your attention to the performance(s) that you are going to use as part of your Controlled Assessment.

This could be:
- a film (seen at the cinema or on DVD)
- an audio CD version
- a live performance.

One possible approach to the study of this part of the unit is given below:
- Try to watch or listen to the performance with as few breaks as possible in order to gain a clear impression of the overall impact and effect of the performance.
- As you are watching or listening, make brief notes on any points that strike you about the performance.
- Think about how the production interprets the text (e.g. does it change the storyline in any way? Are characters presented in a way that you find unusual?).
- Look at the set, costume and the effects created by lighting.

Preparing your notes

During the research and preparation stage of the Controlled Assessment you can prepare some notes that you can refer to when writing your final assignment. You are also allowed to have with you a 'clean copy' of the text (no notes or annotations in it).

Your notes must:
- not contain a full or partly written draft of your assignment
- have been prepared entirely by you, without help from anyone else.

Your notes may be handwritten or typed. Your teacher will check your notes to make sure that they are suitable before you go into your Controlled Assessment.

What your notes can contain

Your notes can include:
- the exact title of your task
- page references for particular parts of the text you want to refer to while writing your assignment
- key quotations
- the names of characters you will focus on
- points to jog your memory
- spellings of particular words.

Look at the sample task below.

Romeo and Juliet

Remind yourself of Act 1, Scene 4 and Act 3, Scene 1 in the text and in one or two performed versions of the play.

Using these scenes as a starting point, and referring to Shakespeare's text as a whole, explore how the characters of Mercutio and Tybalt are portrayed in the performed version(s) you have studied.

You should consider:

- the thoughts and feelings that Mercutio and Tybalt express
- the way the other characters react to them
- the dramatic effect of the scenes and their implications for the rest of the play.

The type of notes shown below would be acceptable.

Notes on the characters Mercutio and Tybalt

Scenes
- Tybalt's attitude to Romeo (Act 1, Scene 5, L53–91)
- Tybalt and Romeo fight (Act 3, Scene 1, L35–135)
- Consequences of conflict – climax (Act 5, Scene 1)
- Pointlessness of conflict - Montague/Capulet/Prince's closing words (Act 5, Scene 1)
- Mercutio's 'joky' nature and his attitude to love and Romeo (Act 1, Scene 4)
- Mercutio's attitude towards Tybalt (Act 3, Scene 1)

Quotations

"Tybalt: This by his voice should be a Montague...
          Now by the stock and honour of my kin.
          To strike him dead I hold it not a sin"
(Act 1, Scene 5, L53–58)

"Tybalt: Romeo, the love I bear thee can afford
          No better term than this – thou art a villain"
(Act 3, Scene 1, L61–62)

"Mercutio: If love be rough with you, be rough with love.
           Prick love for pricking, and you beat love down."
(Act 1, Scene 4, L25–26)

"Mercutio: O calm, dishonourable, vile submission!
           Alla stoccata carries it away.
           Tybalt, you rat-catcher, will you walk?"
(Act 3, Scene 1, L74–76)

R AND J FILM VERSION

Setting – 'Italian style' location – outdoor shots

Change in film from text – at ball Tybalt runs to Lord Capulet to complain about R's presence – different from text – why?

Mercutio –'joker' element really highlighted

Tybalt - portrayed as very serious with 'dangerous' feel about him.

Change in film from text – in fight Mercutio dies in front of R – how does this change the effect from text? Why the change?

Literary heritage poetry

Studying your poems

A key element in this part of your Controlled Assessment is to 'make links and comparisons between texts'. You will need to compare **two** poems by your chosen poet.

Before you can compare the poems, you need to study them closely to gain a clear and detailed understanding of them. A planned approach will ensure you study all aspects of your chosen poems thoroughly.

Here is one method you could use.

1. Look carefully at the choice of tasks and consider all the themes and ideas involved.
2. Look at the set poems by each poet and read each one through. While doing this, keep in mind that you are going to compare the poems, so look out for any similarities or links you can see between them as you read.
3. Select the task that you are going to focus on for your Controlled Assessment.
4. Re-read the relevant poems several times and make brief notes on each.
5. Now you can begin to look at each poem in more detail. You need to look carefully at these elements.

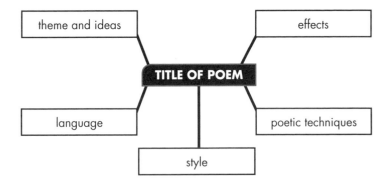

Comparing poems

When you have arrived at a detailed understanding of each of
the poems you will compare, you are ready to start planning your
comparison.

Comparing is all about making connections between poems.
* First, find what the two poems have in common.
* Then consider contrasting attitudes, viewpoints and stylistic
  techniques.

Consider the points of comparison below:
* The **content** of the poems – what they are about.
* How **characters** are used and presented in the poems.
* The **ideas** the poets may want you to think about.
* The ways in which **language** and imagery is used to create effects.
* The **poetic techniques** used and the effects they create.
* The **mood** or **atmosphere** of the poems.
* The way they are **structured** and **organised**.
* How you **respond** to the poems.

You can write your comparison either by:
1. writing about each poem separately and then comparing them
   (if you use this method make sure that your comparisons are
   well-developed in the final section of your response), or
2. making comparisons where appropriate throughout your
   answer as a whole.

When writing comparatively there are certain words and phrases
that you can use to help you structure your response. Some of them
are listed below.

These suggest differences:
* on the other hand...
* however...
* compared with...
* in contrast to...
* whereas...
* unlike...

These suggest similarities:
* similarly...
* likewise...
* in the same way...
* equally...

Using some of these words or phrases in your work will help you
develop and structure your ideas in a comparative way.

Preparing your notes

You are allowed the same amount of time for preparing, researching and writing your poetry assessment as you are allowed for your Shakespeare work:

- **16–20 hours** of preparation
- **4–6 hours** of research time
- up to **3 hours** to complete your final piece of **1000 words**.

The following is an example of the kind of task you might be set and some of the kinds of notes that would be acceptable.

Poems: 'Drummer Hodge' and 'The Man He Killed' by Thomas Hardy

Compare the ways in which Hardy portrays the effects of war in these poems.

You should consider:

- the situations Hardy describes
- the feelings he portrays
- the language he uses.

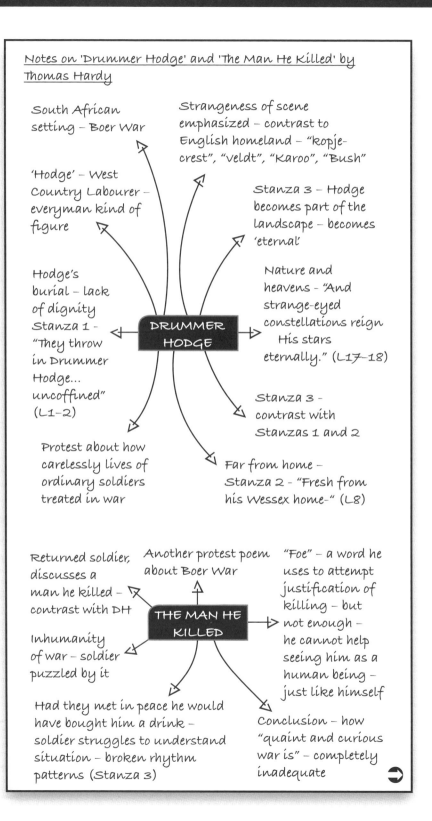

Notes on 'Drummer Hodge' and 'The Man He Killed' by Thomas Hardy

South African setting – Boer War

Strangeness of scene emphasized – contrast to English homeland – "kopje-crest", "veldt", "Karoo", "Bush"

'Hodge' – West Country Labourer – everyman kind of figure

Stanza 3 – Hodge becomes part of the landscape – becomes 'eternal'

Hodge's burial – lack of dignity Stanza 1 - "They throw in Drummer Hodge... uncoffined" (L1–2)

Nature and heavens - "And strange-eyed constellations reign His stars eternally." (L17–18)

DRUMMER HODGE

Stanza 3 - contrast with Stanzas 1 and 2

Protest about how carelessly lives of ordinary soldiers treated in war

Far from home – Stanza 2 - "Fresh from his Wessex home-" (L8)

Returned soldier, discusses a man he killed – contrast with DH

Another protest poem about Boer War

"Foe" – a word he uses to attempt justification of killing – but not enough – he cannot help seeing him as a human being – just like himself

THE MAN HE KILLED

Inhumanity of war – soldier puzzled by it

Had they met in peace he would have bought him a drink – soldier struggles to understand situation – broken rhythm patterns (Stanza 3)

Conclusion – how "quaint and curious war is" – completely inadequate

Similarities	Differences
Topic	Context
Poet's view of war	Tone
Lack of overt judgemental comment	Structure
	Rhythm
Message is the way poet presents ideas – language	Viewpoint/poetic voice
	Language
Conclusion	

You might then follow your notes with a plan of how you are going to structure your comparative essay.

Boost your grade

In order to achieve the best possible grade in this unit you must:

* know your texts very well
* demonstrate a clear understanding of what the texts are about
* be able to give your opinion on characters, setting and themes
* understand how drama texts can be interpreted differently on stage and film
* understand how writers use language and dramatic and stylistic features to create effects
* be able to analyse and comment on the effects achieved
* compare poetry texts effectively
* use details from the text to support and illustrate your ideas
* be able to present your ideas clearly and logically.

Shakespeare and film/audio/live performance

To achieve the best grade you will need to:

* show a sophisticated critical response when interpreting your chosen Shakespeare play and the performed version(s)
* make references to the text using carefully selected and relevant details
* show a convincing and precise evaluation of relevant detail from your Shakespeare play and the performed version(s)
* evaluate the relationships, attitudes and motives of characters
* convey your ideas and put your points across in a persuasive and clear way.

Literary heritage poetry

To achieve the best grade you will need to:

* write a sustained discussion of the links and comparisons between the texts
* show a perceptive exploration and explanation of a wide range of points of connection between your chosen texts
* show sensitive and discriminating analysis in comparing ways in which meaning and effects are created in your texts
* select appropriate detail from the texts to cross-reference your ideas.

Exam insight

Unit Summary

This unit is worth 25% of your overall GCSE English Literature mark.

Unit 2: Modern Drama

Unit 2 is assessed through an external exam (45 minutes)

You will study **one** modern drama text chosen from the set text list provided by OCR:
- *The History Boys:* Alan Bennett
- *Hobson's Choice:* Harold Brighouse
- *A View from the Bridge:* Arthur Miller
- *An Inspector Calls:* J. B. Priestley
- *Educating Rita:* Willy Russell
- *Journey's End:* R.C. Sherriff

You will answer **one** question chosen from two offered on the text you have studied.

One of these questions will be based on an extract from the drama text you have studied and you will need to consider the dramatic build up of this extract and its relation to the play as a whole. The second question will focus on an aspect of the play that allows you to range more widely, making comment, criticism and analysis.

This is an open book exam so you are allowed to take a copy of the text you have studied into the exam with you. Your text must **not** contain any notes or annotations.

Assessment Objectives

This unit will test the following Assessment Objectives:

AO1 Critical response to texts

AO1

Respond to texts critically and imaginatively; select and evaluate relevant textual detail to illustrate and support interpretations.

This means that you will need to show in your answer that you have read your texts closely and are able to analyse aspects of them such as the relationships, attitudes and motives of characters. You will need to use carefully selected details from the text to illustrate and support your ideas.

AO2 Analysing language, structure and form

AO2

Explain how language, structure and form contribute to writers' presentations of ideas, themes and settings.

This means that you will look at the different ways writers use language to achieve effects and analyse stylistic features to show how these affect meaning.

Approaching your drama text

When studying a drama text it is important to bear in mind that they are usually written to be seen in performance rather than read in a classroom.

It will really help your study of the text if you can see a performance of it. If you cannot see a live performance of it on stage, try to watch it on DVD or listen to a recording of it.

The plan below suggests one way you could approach the study of your play.
1. Read the whole play. Reading it aloud with others taking parts will help to bring the play to life. Making brief notes or summaries of scenes is a useful way to get an overall picture of the plot and characters.

2. Once you have read the play you can look it in more detail. You could:
   - think about the ideas or themes explored in the play
   - think about how the play is structured – the way that the events of the plot link together
   - make notes on the characters – who they are, what they do
   - look at the key speeches of the main characters
   - think about the dramatic effects and how the dramatist creates them
   - look carefully at the language of the play, including the dialogue and soliloquies and what these reveal about characters and themes
   - look at the stage directions and what they tell you.

3. Finally, make more detailed notes on the play. You could:
   - create Act/Scene summaries
   - track key ideas and themes
   - keep a character log with notes on key characters and significant quotations
   - identify key speeches
   - highlight language use, imagery and symbolism.

Opening scenes

The opening of a play is very important because a writer must capture the audience's interest and attention straight away.
For example, the opening scene can:

- give background information or an explanation of what has gone on before the play opens
- create a setting or background against which the action of the play is set
- establish a particular mood or atmosphere, for example a sense of tension
- introduce a key character or characters
- create a sense of mystery to intrigue the audience and make them want to know more.

The key questions you need to ask yourself when looking at the opening scene are:

- What effect does the writer want this scene to have on the audience?
- What purpose does the scene serve in the context of the play as a whole?

Look carefully at the opening scene of the play you are studying.

Make notes on:
- how the play opens
- what you think the writer wants to achieve here
- what effect it has on the audience.

Analysing characters

The points below suggest things to look for when analysing the characters in the play, you are studying.

Stage directions
Sometimes dramatists give important information about their characters in stage directions. When studying a play you will read these directions, but when watching a play you will see how these translate into visual effects or action.

Modern Drama

Dialogue

What the characters say will be of key importance. Consider how closely the characters' words match up with their actions and what the characters say about each other. Look at:

- how characters speak (sometimes indicated by stage directions)
- how other characters respond to them and what they say about them

Soliloquies and asides

Both these techniques can reveal the inner thoughts and feelings of a character.

- **Asides** are short comments that are spoken by a character so that other characters cannot hear them but the audience can. Dramatists can use this technique to give small pieces of information about plot or character to the audience. Asides can also reveal things about the character speaking.
- **Soliloquies** are usually longer and more developed speeches where the character is alone on stage or at least out of earshot of other characters on stage. Dramatists often use soliloquies to grant the audience an insight into the deepest throughts of a character.

Think about the key characters in the play you are studying.

Make a character 'log' for each character in which you record key points about their actions, traits and development in the play together with evidence to support and illustrate your points.

You could record the information in a grid like the one below to help when you come to revise.

Character:		
Act/scene	**Point**	**Evidence/quotation**

Exploring themes

Almost all plays explore wider ideas or issues in some way. You should try to identify what these key ideas or themes are early on in your study of the play.

Here are some ways in which dramatists can present themes:
- through the dialogue that occurs between characters
- through what the characters do, how they behave and relate to each other
- through key speeches in the play
- through the use of imagery and symbolism
- through the use of setting.

Think about the themes explored in the play that you are studying and write about:

- what you think the main theme is in the play
- the way this theme is presented in the play.

Make sure that you look at the full range of methods and techniques the dramatist uses to present the theme. Remember to support your ideas with references from the text.

Setting, mood and atmosphere

As a play is meant to be seen rather than read, the setting, mood and atmosphere can be suggested and established in various ways.

The list below suggests key points to think about when considering how the setting is important to the play as a whole or how mood and atmosphere are created by the dramatist.

- **The language** – what characters say and how they say it can set the tone and therefore create a sense of mood and atmosphere.
- **The stage set** gives a sense of setting and can suggest a particular atmosphere. (When reading the text, this kind of information is given in the form of stage directions.) In some plays stage directions are very detailed, in others they are more minimal.

- **Lighting** can be used to create all kinds of effects and can influence the mood and atmosphere enormously.
- **Sound effects** can also add greatly to the impact of the drama, for example, when creating a storm scene, lighting and sound can combine to create a vivid sense of the scene. Music too can be an important feature.
- **Props** can be used in different ways to add effect.

Remember: when analysing the dramatic techniques used to create a sense of setting, mood or atmosphere, look at how all the features combine to produce an overall effect.

Think about the text you are studying and choose an extract (about 30–40 lines) that you feel creates a strong sense of mood and atmosphere.

With close reference to the extract, show how the dramatist creates mood and atmosphere for an audience here.

Boost your grade

In order to achieve the best possible grade in this unit you must:
- know your texts very well
- demonstrate a clear understanding of what the texts are about
- be able to give your opinions on characters, context, setting and themes
- understand how drama texts can be interpreted on stage and in film
- understand how writers use language and dramatic and stylistic features to create effects
- be able to analyse and comment on the effects achieved
- use details from the text to support and illustrate your ideas
- be able to present your ideas clearly and logically.

Your work will be marked on how well you meet the demands of the Assessment Objectives AO1 and AO2.

AO1 Critical response to texts

To achieve the best grade you will need to:
- show a sophisticated critical response when interpreting your chosen play
- make references to the text using carefully selected and relevant details
- show a convincing and precise evaluation of relevant detail from the play
- evaluate the attitudes, motives and relationships of characters
- understand how dramatists use ideas, themes and settings and show the effect these have on the audience
- convey your ideas and put your points across in a persuasive and clear way.

AO2 Analysing language, structure and form

To achieve the best grade you will need to:
- show a sensitive understanding of the significance and effects of the dramatist's choices of language, structure and form
- understand how dramatists use language to achieve their effects
- explore and evaluate the meaning of the play
- understand how language, structure and form are used to present ideas, themes and settings
- analyse stylistic features of the texts.

Unit 3
Prose from Different Cultures

Exam insight

Unit Summary

This unit is worth 25% of your overall GCSE English Literature mark.

Unit 3: Prose from Different Cultures

Unit 3 is assessed through an external exam (45 minutes)

You will study **one** prose text from a different culture chosen from the set text list provided by OCR:

* *Of Mice and Men:* John Steinbeck
* *To Kill a Mockingbird:* Harper Lee
* *Anita and Me:* Meera Syal
* *The Joy Luck Club:* Amy Tan
* *Paddy Clarke Ha Ha Ha:* Roddy Doyle
* *Tsotsi*: Athol Fugard

You will answer **one** question chosen from two offered on the text you have studied.

One of these questions will be based on an extract from the prose text you have studied and will ask you to focus on an aspect of this in your answer. The second question will focus on an aspect of the text that allows you to range more widely, making comment, criticism and analysis.

This is an open book exam so you are allowed to take a copy of the text you have studied into the exam with you. You text must **not** contain any notes or annotations.

Assessment Objectives

This unit will test the following Assessment Objectives:

AO2

Explain how language, structure and form contribute to writers' presentations of ideas, themes and settings.

This means that you will analyse stylistic features and look at the different ways writers use language to achieve effects.

AO4

Relate texts to their social, cultural and historical contexts; explain how texts have been influential and significant to self and other readers in different contexts and at different times

This means that you will examine how different factors, such as the historical period or social or cultural factors can influence the way a text is written and how it affects the reader.

Approaching your text

The term 'different cultures' is a very broad one and can cover a whole range of very different cultures from all over the world.

The prose text that you study for this unit will have much in common with other prose texts that you have studied. However you might find that it:

- is set in a context that is different from those you are familiar with
- presents different lifestyles and ideas
- presents different values or ways of life
- uses non-standard English or dialect forms to reflect the particular cultural background it focuses on.

Prose from Different Cultures

Understanding the plot and storyline

Whatever kind of prose text you are studying, your first task is to read your text in order to get a clear idea of the plot or storyline.

Consider the suggestions below to help you develop your understanding of the text.

1   Read through the whole text to get a full sense of the plot.
2   Write a brief summary of the key points of the plot and the central characters in the story.

To develop a full sense of the plot, you need to have a clear understanding of it structure and how the events of the novel and the characters relate to one other.

Consider the list of points below and bear these in mind as you study your text for this unit.

*   What is the narrative viewpoint – is the story told from a first- or third-person perspective?
*   Know the characters – who they are, what they do, how they relate to each other, what they do in the story and how the writer presents them.
*   Look at the setting and context of the story – think about where and when it is set.
*   Look closely at how the writer uses language to create particular effects, present characters and describe settings.

As you read your text you should make notes which will help you with your studies and revision later. Here are some things you might make notes on:

*   key events in the story
*   character traits and relationships
*   the setting and how this links to key themes in the novel
*   passages, descriptions and quotations that you find interesting or effective.

Analysing characters

Characters are a key element in any novel and writers use a variety of techniques to present them to the reader. It is important that a writer creates characters that we, as readers, find convincing and believable.

Prose from Different Cultures

The list below suggests some of the ways that writers can present their characters.

- **Description** – writers can tell you what the characters look like, how they are dressed, how they walk and how they talk. They can also describe their physical characteristics.
- **Speech** – writers often use speech to reveal important information about characters. Look not only at **what** the characters say but also **how** they say it. What other characters say about a particular character can also be important.
- **Actions and behaviour** – how characters behave can help to build up a picture of them.
- **Thoughts and feelings** – writers often tell you what characters are thinking or feeling.
- **Imagery and symbols** – writers sometimes link characters to particular symbols or use particular images to describe them. For example, in *Of Mice and Men*, Steinbeck often uses animal imagery to describe Lennie, who is a huge, powerful man.

When you analyse how characters are presented, you should look at:
- what they do
- how they behave and react to situations
- what they say and how they say it
- what other characters say about them
- how they react and relate to other characters
- the ways the writer uses language to present them.

Read the extract that follows from the opening of *Of Mice and Men* by John Steinbeck.

The first man was small and quick, dark of face, with restless eyes and sharp, strong features. Every part of him was defined: small, strong hands, slender arms, a thin and bony nose. Behind him walked his opposite, a huge man, shapeless of face, with large, pale eyes, with wide, sloping shoulders; and he walked heavily, dragging his feet a little, the way a bear drags his paws. His arms did not swing at his sides, but hung loosely. ⮕

➡ The first man stopped short in the clearing, and the follower nearly ran over him. He took off his hat and wiped the sweatband with his forefinger and snapped the moisture off. His huge companion dropped his blankets and flung himself down and drank from the surface of the green pool; drank with long gulps, snorting into the water like a horse. The small man stepped nervously beside him.

"Lennie!" he said sharply. "Lennie, for God' sakes don't drink so much." Lennie continued to snort into the pool. The small man leaned over and shook him by the shoulder. "Lennie. You gonna be sick like you was last night."

Lennie dipped his whole head under, hat and all, and then he sat up on the bank and his hat dripped down on his blue coat and ran down his back. "Tha's good," he said. "You drink some, George. You take a good big drink." He smiled happily.

George unslung his bindle and dropped it gently on the bank. "I ain't sure it's good water," he said. "Looks kinda scummy."

Lennie dabbled his big paw in the water and wiggled his fingers so the water arose in little splashes; rings widened across the pool to the other side and came back again. Lennie watched them go. "Look, George. Look what I done."

From the extract above what impression do you form of:
a. George
b. Lennie?

You should look at:
- how Steinbeck uses language to describe each character
- how each character behaves
- how the characters respond to each other
- what the characters say and how they say it.

Use specific examples from the extract to illustrate your points.

Setting and context

The setting and context of a novel is important for several reasons:
- it forms the physical background against which the events of the novel take place
- it provides the circumstances or situation in which the plot and develops
- it can portray a particular view of a 'society' and can be linked to particular values or themes.

The grid below provides notes on the settings and contexts of all the set novels for this unit. Look for the text you are studying.

Novel	Setting and context
Of Mice and Men	Set in California during the Great Depression, it focuses on the lives of two migrant ranch workers.
To Kill a Mockingbird	Set in a small town in Alabama in the American Deep South during the 1930s, it relates the experiences of a young girl growing up in a society affected by racism and prejudice.
Anita and Me	Set in a Midlands mining village in the 1970s, it focuses on the experiences of a Punjabi girl growing up in that area.
The Joy Luck Club	Set in San Francisco, California, it focuses on four Chinese American immigrant families who start a club called The Joy Luck Club which involves playing the game of mah-jong for money.
Paddy Clarke Ha Ha Ha	Set in Ireland in the 1960s, it explores the events and memories of a ten-year-old boy growing up at that time.
Tsosti	Set in a black African township in Johannesburg, South Africa, it tells the story of a street thug and is set against a background of violence and racism.

Look at the passage below which comes from the opening of *To Kill a Mockingbird* by Harper Lee.

1. What overall impression does the writer give of the town?
2. Pick out any words or phrases that you think are particularly effective in creating a sense of the setting.

Maycomb was an old town, but it was a tired old town when I first knew it. In rainy weather the streets turned to <u>red</u> slop; grass grew on the sidewalks, the court-house sagged in the square. Somehow, it was hotter then; a black dog suffered on a summer's day; bony mules hitched to Hoover carts flicked flies in the sweltering shade of the live oaks on the square. Men's stiff collars wilted by nine in the morning. Ladies bathed before noon, after their three o'clock naps, and by nightfall were like soft teacakes with frostings of sweat and sweet talcum.

People moved slowly then. They ambled across the square, shuffled in and out of the stores around it, took their time about everything. A day was twenty-four hours long but seemed longer. There was no hurry, for there was nowhere to go, nothing to buy and no money to buy it with, nothing to see outside the boundaries of Maycomb County.

Now think about the text that you are studying.

1. Pick out **three** passages from the novel and read them carefully.
2. Analyse the ways in which the writer uses language to give a strong impression, picture or feeling about the setting and atmosphere.

Remember to use specific details from the text to support and illustrate your ideas.

Prose from Different Cultures

Exploring themes

Themes are the ideas that a writer might explore through the novel. Often a writer might want to draw attention to particular ideas or issues so that the reader will think about them. Sometimes writers want to put across particular messages about the issues they explore.

When you are studying your novel it is a good idea to make a list of the main themes or ideas that you identify. It may help you to use a diagram, like the one shown below, to summarize your ideas.

This diagram relates to the key themes in *Of Mice and Men*.

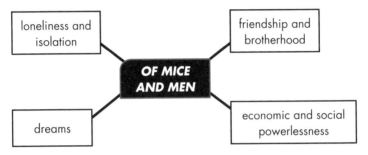

Make a list of four key themes that are explored in the novel you are studying.

Make brief notes on the ideas that are suggested and any messages that you think the writer wants to make the reader think about.

Having established what you see as the key themes in your novel you now need to look at each one in more detail.

The list below suggests some things to think about:
- How does each theme relate to the main storyline?
- What message does the writer want to convey to the reader?
- How does the writer present the themes? You should look at:
  - the language used
  - the use of imagery
  - the use of symbols or motifs.

Remember that you should use specific examples from the text to support and illustrate the points you make.

When making notes on themes it can be useful to include page references so that you can find the relevant sections easily when you are revising.

Look back at the novel you are studying and use a grid, like the one below, to develop your ideas on the key themes you have identified using examples from the text.

Theme	How it is presented	Examples of language

Boost your grade

In order to achieve the best possible grade in this unit you must:
- know your texts very well
- be able to give your opinion about characters, context, setting and themes
- understand how the writer uses language and stylistic features to create effects
- analyse and comment on the effects achieved
- use details from the text to support and illustrate your ideas
- be able to present your ideas clearly and logically.

Your work will be marked on how well you meet the demands of the Assessment Objectives AO2 and AO4.

AO2 Analysing language, structure and form

To achieve the best grade you will need to:
- show a sensitive understanding of the significance and effects of writers' choices of language, structure and form
- show a clear and perceptive understanding of the ways in which the writer presents ideas, themes and settings
- explore and evaluate the meanings of texts
- select relevant details to support and illustrate your ideas.

AO4 Social, cultural and historical contexts

To achieve the best grade you will need to:
- present a perceptive exploration and critical evaluation of a wide range of links between texts and their contexts
- be aware of the significance of texts to readers in different contexts
- understand how the texts have been an important influence over time
- be able to relate texts to your own and others' experiences
- understand how details from the texts relate to their social, cultural and historical contexts.

Unit 4
Literary Heritage Prose and Contemporary Poetry

Exam insight

Unit Summary

This unit is worth 25% of your overall GCSE English Literature mark. It is divided into two areas of study.

Unit 4: Literary Heritage Prose and Contemporary Poetry

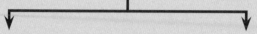

Literary Heritage Prose	**Contemporary Poetry**
(15% of marks)	(10% of marks)

Unit 4 is assessed through an external exam (1 hour 30 minutes)

Literary heritage prose

For the first part of this unit you will study **one** literary heritage prose text chosen from the set text list provided by OCR:

- *Pride and Prejudice:* Jane Austen
- *Silas Marner:* George Eliot
- *The Lord of the Flies:* William Golding
- *The Withered Arm and other Wessex Tales:* Thomas Hardy
- *Animal Farm:* George Orwell
- *The Strange Case of Dr Jekyll and Mr Hyde:* R. L. Stevenson

In the exam you will answer **one** question chosen from two offered on the text you have studied.

One of these questions will be based on an extract from the prose text you have studied and will ask you to focus on an aspect of this in your answer. The second question will focus on an aspect of the text that allows you to range more widely, making comment, criticism and analysis.

This is an open book exam so you are allowed to take a copy of the text you have studied into the exam with you. Your text must **not** contain any notes or annotations.

Contemporary poetry

For the second part of this unit you will study the poetry of **one** of the poets chosen from the list of poets for study provided by OCR:

- Simon Armitage
- Gillian Clarke
- Wendy Cope
- Seamus Heaney
- Carol Ann Duffy
- Benjamin Zephaniah

In the exam you will:

Either

Answer **one** question requiring a response to **one** poem from the poet you have studied. (Three questions will be set on each poet.)

The questions will either be poem-based, or require comment, criticism and analysis.

Or

You will answer **one** question on an unseen contemporary poem.

Assessment Objectives

Both questions in this unit test the following Assessment Objectives:

AO1 Critical response to texts

AOI

Respond to texts critically and imaginatively; select and evaluate relevant textual detail to illustrate and support interpretations.

This means that you will need to show in your answer that you have read your texts carefully and are able to analyse aspects of them such as characters, relationships attitudes and motives. You will need to use carefully selected details from the texts to illustrate and support your ideas.

AO2 Analysing language, structure and form

AO2

Explain how language, structure and form contribute to writers' presentation of ideas, themes and settings.

This means that you will look at the different ways writers use language to achieve effects and analyse stylistic features to show how these affect meaning.

Literary heritage prose

Literary heritage prose texts are texts that have been recognised as important and significant over a period of time and have become established as part of our literary history.

In studying a prose text from the literary heritage your approach will be much the same and have much in common with your study of other prose texts, including the text from a different culture which you studied in Unit 3.

Narrative viewpoint

All the literary heritage texts on the OCR list use third person narration. The extract that follows from *Silas Marner* by George Eliot gives an example of this kind of narration.

It was fifteen years since Silas Marner had first come to Raveloe; he was then simply a pallid young man, with prominent short-sighted brown eyes, whose appearance would have had nothing strange for people of average culture and experience, but for the villagers near whom he had come to settle it had mysterious peculiarities which corresponded with the exceptional nature of his occupation, and his advent from an unknown region called "North'ard". So had his way of life:—he invited no comer to step across his door-sill, and he never strolled into the village to drink a pint at the Rainbow, or to gossip at the wheelwright's: he sought no man or woman, save for the purposes of his calling, or in order to supply himself with necessaries; and it was soon clear to the Raveloe lasses that he would never urge one of them to accept him against her will—quite as if he had heard them declare that they would never marry a dead man come to life again.

Notice here how George Eliot tells her story as if she is able to observe everything that is going on, including how the character behaves and even feels. The narrator is all seeing and all knowing. This kind of narrator is sometimes called the **omniscient narrator**.

Analysing characters

Look at the extract from *Pride and Prejudice* by Jane Austen on the next page and answer the following question.

What methods does Jane Austen use to present the character of Mr Darcy and to shape her reader's response to him.

Mr. Bingley was good-looking and gentlemanlike; he had a pleasant countenance, and easy, unaffected manners. His sisters were fine women, with an air of decided fashion. His brother-in-law, Mr. Hurst, merely looked the gentleman; but his friend Mr. Darcy soon drew the attention of the room by his fine, tall person, handsome features, noble mien, and the report which was in general circulation within five minutes after his entrance, of his having ten thousand a year. The gentlemen pronounced him to be a fine figure of a man, the ladies declared he was much handsomer than Mr. Bingley, and he was looked at with great admiration for about half the evening, till his manners gave a disgust which turned the tide of his popularity; for he was discovered to be proud; to be above his company, and above being pleased; and not all his large estate in Derbyshire could then save him from having a most forbidding, disagreeable countenance, and being unworthy to be compared with his friend.

Mr. Bingley had soon made himself acquainted with all the principal people in the room; he was lively and unreserved, danced every dance, was angry that the ball closed so early, and talked of giving one himself at Netherfield. Such amiable qualities must speak for themselves. What a contrast between him and his friend! Mr. Darcy danced only once with Mrs. Hurst and once with Miss Bingley, declined being introduced to any other lady, and spent the rest of the evening in walking about the room, speaking occasionally to one of his own party. His character was decided. He was the proudest, most disagreeable man in the world, and everybody hoped that he would never come there again. Amongst the most violent against him was Mrs. Bennet, whose dislike of his general behaviour was sharpened into particular resentment by his having slighted one of her daughters.

Elizabeth Bennet had been obliged, by the scarcity of gentlemen, to sit down for two dances; and during part of that time, Mr. Darcy had been standing near enough for her to hear a conversation between him and Mr. Bingley, who came from the dance for a few minutes, to press his friend to join it.

"Come, Darcy," said he, "I must have you dance. I hate to see you standing about by yourself in this stupid manner. You had much better dance."

"I certainly shall not. You know how I detest it, unless I am particularly acquainted with my partner. At such an assembly as this it would be insupportable. Your sisters are engaged, and there is not another woman in the room whom it would not be a punishment to me to stand up with."

Now think about the text you are studying and choose an extract of about 30 lines from it in which a character or characters are a key feature.

Write a response to this question:

Look closely at how the writer of your text presents your chosen character(s) in the extract you have selected. How does it influence the reader's attitude to him/her?

Setting, mood and atmosphere

The mood and atmosphere of a novel (or a short story) is often closely linked to the setting, as well as the feelings and actions of the characters.

Writers often use stylistic techniques and careful language choices to create a sense of mood and atmosphere.

The list below suggests some of the techniques writers can use to achieve their effects.
- Vocabulary choices – using particular words to suggest a particular mood.
- Use of syntax – various lengths and types of sentences can create different effects.
- Dialogue – speech not only conveys information but can also establish a specific tone.
- Repetition of word and phrases.
- Imagery – including similes, metaphors and personification.
- Phonological features – including alliteration, onomatopoeia and assonance.
- Symbols and motifs – words, ideas or images which are repeatedly used in the text.
- Use of the senses, such as smell, touch or sound.

Look at the extract on the next page from *Silas Marner* by George Eliot and answer the following question:

How does the writer use language to create a sense of setting and atmosphere here? Use specific details of language to illustrate and support your ideas.

And Raveloe was a village where many of the old echoes lingered, undrowned by new voices. Not that it was one of those barren parishes lying on the outskirts of civilization—inhabited by meagre sheep and thinly-scattered shepherds: on the contrary, it lay in the rich central plain of what we are pleased to call Merry England, and held farms which, speaking from a spiritual point of view, paid highly-desirable tithes. But it was nestled in a snug well-wooded hollow, quite an hour's journey on horseback from any turnpike, where it was never reached by the vibrations of the coach-horn, or of public opinion. It was an important-looking village, with a fine old church and large churchyard in the heart of it, and two or three large brick-and-stone homesteads, with well-walled orchards and ornamental weathercocks, standing close upon the road, and lifting more imposing fronts than the rectory, which peeped from among the trees on the other side of the churchyard:—a village which showed at once the summits of its social life, and told the practised eye that there was no great park and manor-house in the vicinity, but that there were several chiefs in Raveloe who could farm badly quite at their ease, drawing enough money from their bad farming, in those war times, to live in a rollicking fashion, and keep a jolly Christmas, Whitsun, and Easter tide.

Now think about the text that you are studying.

1. Select an extract of about 30 lines from the novel or short story which you think presents setting and atmosphere effectively.
2. With close reference to the extract, explain how the writer creates a sense of setting, mood and atmosphere.

Themes

Remember, themes are the ideas or messages that a writer might explore in their text. A novel or short story might explore one key theme or it might explore several. Often a writer might want to draw attention to particular ideas or issues so that a reader will think about them.

Think about the key themes presented in the text you are studying and make a list of them.

Pick the theme that you think is most important and explain how the writer presents this theme to the reader, using references to the text to support your points.

Contemporary poetry

To answer the exam questions effectively, you will need to have a clear sense of what it is you should be looking for and you will also need a good grasp of what each poem is about. The following steps show how you might approach this in your exam.

1. Read the question. Make sure that you are completely clear about what the question asks you to do.
2. Next, read through the poem.
3. Make sure that you understand what the poem is about.
4. Go back to the question and think about the poem in relation to the question.
5. As you answer the question, keep in mind:
   - the mood or atmosphere of the poem
   - how the poem is written – words and phrases that you find interesting, the way it is organised and so on
   - your personal response to the poem.

Read the poem below and answer the following question.

How does Duffy present a sense of personal memory in this poem?

Remember to refer closely to the language Duffy uses.

Anne Hathaway

'Item I gyve unto my wife my second best bed...'
(from Shakespeare's will)

The bed we loved in was a spinning world
of forests, castles, torchlight, clifftops, seas
where we would dive for pearls. My lover's words
were shooting stars which fell to earth as kisses
5 on these lips; my body now a softer rhyme
to his, now echo, assonance; his touch
a verb dancing in the centre of a noun.
some nights, I dreamed he'd written me, the bed
a page beneath his writer's hands. Romance
10 and drama played by touch, by scent, by taste.
In the other bed, the best, our guests dozed on,
dribbling their prose. My living laughing love –
I hold him in the casket of my widow's head
as he held me upon that next best bed.

Carol Ann Duffy

The unseen contemporary poem

In Unit 4 you will have the option to answer a question on a previously unseen contemporary poem.

The nature of the unseen option means that you cannot revise any specific poems in advance. What you can do, however, is make sure that by the time you get to the exam, you are well-practiced and confident in using **close reading skills**.

To close read effectively you will need to have a clear sense of what it is you should be looking for and you will also need a good grasp of what the poem is about. The steps on the next page show how you might approach a close reading in your exam.

1. Read the question

The question will ask you things about:

- the **content** of the poem
- how **language** is used
- the **structure** of the poem
- the **effects** created
- any other ideas you think are important.

2. What is the poem about?

When you are dealing with a poem that you have never seen before, the first thing that you need to do is to get a sense of what it is 'about'. Begin by reading through the poem at least twice. Don't worry if you don't understand every word. Your aim is to get an overall impression of the poem: the subject matter, the key themes, and the speaker's perspective. That way, when you look more closely at specific details, you will be aware of how the detail fits together to create the overall effect of the poem.

3. Identify what to look for

Once you have read the poems, you should go back to the question. The question will include a bullet-point list of things that you should look for and could ask you to comment on:

- what the poem is about (you should already have some sense of this following your first read-through)
- the ideas the poet may want you to think about (you will probably have a sense of this too)
- the mood or atmosphere of the poem
- how the poem is written – words and phrases that you find interesting, the way it is organized and so on
- your response to the poem.

4. Annotating the poem

You should now read the poem again and annotate it. Keep the question and bullet points carefully in mind. You could highlight or underline specific words or features that you can comment on in your answer.

Look at the tips below on making useful annotations.

- Mark and comment – Pick out specific words, features and phrases and add a quick word or comment to the margin to say why you have selected it.
- Keep your notes short – your annotations should act as starting points for further thinking, so you should keep them concise and aim to expand and develop them in your written answer.
- Be selective – only pick out the features that stand out or mean something to you. Don't highlight every simile and every metaphor that you find. Only mark features that you can relate to the question. Bear in mind that you will only have about 45 minutes to write your response, so you won't be able to talk about everything.

When you have read your poem and annotated it, think again about these key questions:

- **What** is the poem about?
- **How** does the poet use language in the poem?
- **Why** does the poet use language in the way they do? (The answer to this almost always is to do with the **effects** the poet wants to achieve).

Things to look for

Some suggestions of features you might look for in the poem
you are analysing are given below.

- The vocabulary the poet uses – look at the words they have
  chosen to use and make a note of any words or phrases that
  you find particularly effect and the effects they create.
- Any imagery the poet uses such as:
  - metaphors
  - similes
  - personification
  - aural imagery such as alliteration, onomatopoeia, assonance.
- The use of rhyme.
- The rhythm of the poem.

Remember: just spotting features is not enough – you need to be
able to say something about the **effects** created.

Now practise your close reading skills on the poem on the next
page. Read it through carefully using a planned approach and
then try writing a response to the questions that follow.

My Grandmother

She kept an antique shop – or it kept her.
Among Apostle spoons and Bristol glass,
The faded silks, the heavy furniture,
She watched her own reflection in the brass
5 Salvers and silver bowls, as if to prove
Polish was all, there was no need of love.
And I remember how I once refused
To go out with her, since I was afraid.
It was perhaps a wish not to be used
10 Like antique objects. Though she never said
That she was hurt, I still could feel the guilt
Of that refusal, guessing how she felt.
Later, too frail to keep a shop, she put
All her best things in one long, narrow room.
15 The place smelt old, of things too long kept shut,
The smell of absences where shadows come
That can't be polished. There was nothing then
To give her own reflection back again.
And when she died I felt no grief at all,
20 Only the guilt of what I once refused.
I walked into her room among the tall
Sideboards and cupboards – things she never used
But needed: and no finger-marks were there,
Only the new dust falling through the air.

Elizabeth Jennings

How does Jennings convey a sense of the speaker's feelings?

You should consider:
- the speaker's attitude toward her grandmother
- her description of the antiques shop (lines 2–5)
- some of the language the poet uses
- the structure of the poem
- anything else that you think is important.

Boost your grade

In order to achieve the best possible grade in this unit you must:
- know your texts very well
- analyse the texts you have studied carefully
- demonstrate a clear understanding of what the texts are about
- be aware of the ideas and themes that the writers explore in the texts and how language is used to present these
- explain what you think about the characters, context, setting and atmosphere
- be aware of how to approach the detailed study of poetry
- explain how language and structure are used in texts
- use details from the texts to support and illustrate your ideas.

AO1 Critical response to texts

To achieve the best grade you will need to:
- show a sophisticated critical response when interpreting your chosen text
- make references to the text using carefully selected and relevant details
- evaluate the attitudes, motives and relationships of characters
- understand how writers use ideas, themes and settings and show the effects these have on the reader

AO2 Analysing language, structure and form

To achieve the best grade you will need to:
- show a sensitive understanding of the significance and effects of writers' choices of language, structure and form
- understand how writers use language to achieve their effects
- explore and evaluate the meanings of texts
- understand how language, structure and form are used to present ideas, themes and settings
- analyse stylistic features of the texts.

Glossary

Adjective: a word that describes a noun – e.g. *the wooden table; the red balloon*. They can also indicate degree, e.g. *the tallest girl was the slowest*.

Adverb: a word that describes the action of a verb – e.g. *the boy ate hungrily*.

Allegory: a story or narrative that has a deeper meaning below the surface action, e.g. *Animal Farm* by George Orwell.

Alliteration: the repetition of the same consonant sound, often at the beginning of words. For example, 'five miles meandering with a mazy motion' ('Kubla Khan' by Samuel Taylor Coleridge).

Allusion: a reference to another event, person, place or work of literature to add meaning to the message, idea, point or theme.

Antithesis: contrasting ideas or words that are balanced against each other, e.g. 'To be, or not to be' (*Hamlet* by William Shakespeare).

Assonance: the repetition of similar vowel sounds. For example, 'there must be Gods thrown down and trumpets blown' ('Hyperion' by John Keats). This shows the paired assonance of *must, trum* and *thrown, blown.*

Atmosphere: the mood created by a piece of writing.

Bathos: an anti-climax or sudden descent from serious to ridiculous.

Blank verse: unrhymed poetry consisting of iambic pentameter (a ten-syllable line consisting of an unstressed syllable followed by a stressed one.

Caesura: a deliberate break in a line of poetry.

Colloquial: slang or non-standard features in speech or writing.

Conjunction: a word that connect words, e.g. *and*, *but*.

Contraction: a shortened word, e.g. *isn't, don't*.

Couplet: two consecutive lines of verse that rhyme.

Dialect: a language variety marked by distinctive grammar and vocabulary, often used by people with a common regional background.

Dialogue: speech between two or more people.

Direct speech: the actual words spoken by a person, recorded in written form using speech marks or quotation marks.

Elegy: a sad, reflective poem often concerned with death.

Empathy: a feeling of understanding or shared experience.

End-stopping: a line of verse with a pause or a stop at the end of it.

Enjambment: a line of verse that flows into the next line without a pause.

Free verse: verse written without any fixed structure.

Genre: a particular kind of writing, e.g. prose, poetry, drama.

Hyperbole: a deliberate and extravagant exaggeration.

Imagery: the use of words to create a picture or 'image' in the mind of the reader. Images can relate to any of the five senses. The term is often used to refer to the use of descriptive language, particularly to the use of **metaphors** and **similes**.

Indirect speech: the words of a speaker that are reported rather than being quoted directly – e.g. *David said that he was going out.* **Direct Speech** would be *'I am going out,' said David.*

Internal rhyme: words that rhyme within a line rather than at the end of lines.

Interrogative: a question.

Intonation: the tone of voice in speech.

Metaphor: a comparison of one thing to another to make description more vivid. Unlike a **simile**, a metaphor states that one thing *is* the other. For example, a simile could be *The wind cut through me like a knife*, whereas the metaphor might state *The wind cut through me.*

Narrative: a piece of writing or speech that tells a story.

Onomatopoeia: the use of words whose sounds copy the sounds of the thing or process they describe. On a simple level, words like *bang, hiss* and *splash* are onomatopoeic.

Oxymoron: a figure of speech which puts together words of opposite meaning, e.g. *bitter sweet.*

Parody: a kind of writing that copies the style of another writer or style of writing, often with the purpose of mocking the original.

Pathos: an effect in writing that makes the reader feel sadness or pity.

Plot: the main storyline, e.g. of a novel or play.

Pun: a play on a word that often have a similar sound but different meanings in order to create a humorous effect.

Purpose: the reason why a piece of writing has been written or a speech made, e.g. to entertain, to explain, to persuade, to argue.

Rhyme scheme: the pattern of rhymes in a poem.

Simile: a comparison of one thing to another in order to make description more vivid. Similes use the words *like* or *as* to make the comparison, e.g. *The ice was like glass under foot.*

Slang: distinctive words and phrases associated with informal speech. Very often it is used within certain social or age groups.

Soliloquy: a speech given by a character alone on stage in which he or she expresses their thoughts and feelings to the audience.

Sonnet: a fourteen-line poem, usually with ten syllables per line.

Stanzas: the groups of lines into which a poem is divided (the correct term for what are sometimes called 'verses').

Structure: the way that a poem, play or other piece of writing has been put together. This can include the metre pattern, stanza arrangement and the ways the ideas are structured developed.

Symbol: like images, symbols are things which represent or indicate something else, e.g. a <u>red</u> rose can symbolize love, or the colour blue can symbolize innocence.

Synonym: different words with the same or similar meanings, e.g. *shut* and *close* or *ship* and *vessel.*

Syntax: the way sentences are structured.

Theme: a central idea or message that a writer explores or presents through a text.

Tone: the tone of a text is created through the combined effects of a number of features, such as vocabulary, syntax and rhythm. The tone can be a major factor in establishing the overall impression of a piece of writing.

Vocabulary: the words of a language.